47 STEPS TO BEING WHO YOU ARE
Tips for Business and Life

BY

DOUG ROSS

authorHOUSE™

1663 LIBERTY DRIVE, SUITE 200
BLOOMINGTON, INDIANA 47403
(800) 839-8640
WWW.AUTHORHOUSE.COM

First published by AuthorHouse 2/14/2006

ISBN: 1-4208-7673-2 (sc)

Library of Congress Control Number: 2005908164

Printed in the United States of America
Bloomington, Indiana

This book is printed on acid-free paper.

"A daily reminder of how to live life happily"

Here are 47 short tips for success and happiness. If you read one a day, there are enough to last you a month and a half! They are written in the spirit of Taoism.

DR   9/99 – 7/05

1. Find out who you are; who have you been? Who are you now? Who will you be? Most of us don't know how to ask for feedback about ourselves. Maybe we don't want to hear some truths. Business leaders have consultants interview stakeholders and then give feedback to the company so it can better itself. People need to do this too. Who are the stakeholders in your life? Who do they say you are?

2. Be honest AND realistic. Be truthful and sensitive, but be sure to be grounded and in touch with reality. The safest way to be honest is to say how you are feeling. The reason for this is that feelings are inside of us. As soon as we say what or who is the cause, there is a good chance that person will feel blamed, so say how you feel and describe the situation that generated the feeling. Being honest is sometimes difficult for others to hear, but if it is an important truth, the longer term outcome will be better.

3. Be idealistic; strive for quality in all you do.   Seek the highest ground.   Don't settle for good enough, do what it takes to be better.   The quality movement in business came about because U.S. companies were not matching the quality of products from Japan and Germany and were losing market share. If you want to keep your market share, do it well the first time. Make it a practice to make excellent products and provide quality service.

4. Treat people well, with courtesy, respect, and caring. Appreciate and honor others. Never be rude, disrespectful, overbearing, unkind, or hostile. Try to understand that people are different, have different values, come from different cultures, have different beliefs. Let it be acceptable to be different.

5. Be grounded, down to earth, straight forward, and authentic. Don't be haughty, and lord it over people. Don't use jargon or pseudo-sophisticated language to attempt to appear better than somebody else. Don't be obtuse; talk straight and stay on the point without wandering off. Be real; be who you really are and be comfortable with who you really are. Businesses identify and publicize their life force and organizing principles to remain clearly focused. They create missions, visions, and values lists and revisit their purposes. You can do that too.

6. When you are working with another person or a group, get agreement on purpose. Take time up front to find out if you are in agreement, and try to work toward joint purpose. Revisit purpose often. See if you both still agree. If it seems like it is unclear, ask, "We are doing this because . . . ?'

7. Agree on a meaningful mission - one that has heart and soul in it. Whether at work or thinking of your own life, write a mission statement and live by it. Find a way to make your work and life meaningful so that you can look back and be proud of yourself. Be sure the mission you write or speak is the mission you live and believe.

8. Especially in business, but in family relationships too, have a clear shared vision. Be sure it is really shared. This means everybody has an equal role in it's creation and will work to make it work. For a flexible shared vision, have scenarios, or backup plans for most eventualities you can imagine. Have alternative plans of action depending on what happens beyond your control.

9. See that your world is changing; ask what risks you are willing to take to keep up with the changes. Change is always with us, inside of us, in our relationships and partnerships, and in the groups we work in. Change is happening around us, whether we like it or not. It is better to surf the front of the wave than be caught in the wash. Embrace change. Take risks that will make change easy for you.

10. Listen attentively to what people are saying. Be open to their ideas. Seek diverse opinions. Do this so that it is second nature to understand that we all are different, and that no one is big enough to know it all. Others' ideas can add to your own. Ask them what they think. Diversity generates creativity, because we are forced to see things in new and different ways. Embrace diversity.

11. Speak from a deep place of wisdom. Trust yourself more than regurgitating what others have said. Filter knowledge through your experience and speak from that wisdom. Get in touch with what things mean to you. This is a way to know who you are. Don't brag, or make promises you can't keep. Find common ground among those you are with. Ask how we are similar; "what do we have in common?"

12. Ask questions that expand possibilities. Invite in more than you know or have said. Be interested in another persons view. Ask how we can make this better. Ask what other reference point would add to what we are thinking about now. Ask questions that begin with, "What if . . . ?"

Doug Ross

13. Encourage creativity. Generate ideas and let them incubate. Try an idea that seems unrelated at first; see whether it adds to the thinking. Invite in the new, the unusual, the different. Rearrange your furniture in a uniquely different way and try it out. You can always return to the old way if it was better.

14. Own your truth and speak it without judging others. Be honest, and be sure you mean what you say. Judgments are born out of needs to be right, to be better than, or more of, or higher than. What if there is no right or wrong, but only what is? What can we learn from differences? Rumi said, "Out beyond wrongdoing and rightdoing, there is a field. I'll meet you there." Meet me in that field.

15. Pay attention to what energizes you. These things are your passion, and you will be easily motivated to engage and do well. If you seem to have no passion in your life or work, please go sit in the warm sun and ask the warmth to raise your passion so you can see it. Ask others what they think you love. What lights up your eyes? What makes you sit on the edge of your seat? What stops you when you are walking past? Get involved in these things to make your life more meaningful.

16. Let go of your pet ideas if others don't like them. Don't always argue to win. We sometimes get caught up in ourselves and think it is important to have the best idea, or the wisest thing to say. We are posturing. Try saying what you think and letting go of the outcome. If others like it, it will be embraced. If they don't, let go. Maybe this is not the time, or the place. Try it again later, or with different people. Find the "win" in what we all want.

17. Appreciate what people do, including you. You can't be appreciated too much if it is authentic. Watch for things people do that you like and compliment them. Notice that you too are worth appreciating. Maybe you need to appreciate yourself to appreciate others. Make a list for yourself of things you appreciate about yourself. Be specific; point out details of your appreciation.

18. Be willing to be passionate when something matters to you. Emotions are a good thing; don't hide them. Find out if you can be passionate and still willing to let go if your idea isn't embraced. You will feel good about yourself for having authentically expressed what is important for you. Be sure to remember to "do no harm".

19. Think of your system. This means don't be narrow-minded. In a business, there are many factors working at once, suppliers, contacts, past reputation, personal relations, visions, internal and external environments, customers, distribution, laws and much, much more. Personal lives are influenced in many ways. Our bodies are themselves complex systems, with rhythms, shapes, strengths and weakness, and a huge variety of states of mind. Open up to all that is around you and how these diverse factors influence you or your business.

20. Give gifts. Small or large, gifts make people happy. Some of your gifts are human gifts, the services you provide, deep listening, experiences you share. Companies give to their communities, give to their employees, contribute to a better world. Give to your self. Make your world better.

21. Don't give up doing what you do best. Think all the way back to your childhood and think about two or three things you have always been good at. Keep doing these things. If you change jobs, move, enter a new relationship, keep doing what you do well and work to improve it. These are your real gifts.

22. "Understand and then seek to be understood." Stephen Covey said this in The Seven Habits of Highly Effective People. What good advice! Listen well and ask questions. If you demonstrate your interest in other people, they will be interested in you! If they are not, you may not be destined to be friends.

23. Plan your work; work your plan. Planning prepares you and makes the way easier to traverse. Implementing it will be easier, even if the plan needs to be revised in mid-course. Some businesses are using scenario planning to generate more than one plan. This is necessary since we don't always know what the future holds for us.

24. Give up rightness and wrongness. Why is it so important to be right? Who cares if somebody thinks differently than us. What if we recall things differently. A key to emerge from these questions is, "Can we agree to disagree?" "There are many ways to skin a cat", a gruesome expression, but a valid one. My friend Jim Long used to say that there are three ways to do anything, the right way, the wrong way, and the Long way!

25. Seek a long-term view. Lift your head and see the horizon. Long views offer more perspective, and sometimes indicate the vastness of the terrain. Long views are valuable to companies who want to stay viable for an extended future fraught with change. Short-term thinking causes trouble. Do you have a quarterly bottom line? Does it keep you thinking about the short run? Stand along an ocean, or on a mountaintop and look out and up. Stand on the brink of the Grand Canyon. Listen to what you are thinking.

26. Mourn losses; then move on. Loss will happen to all of us. It is worth grieving, letting ourselves fully experience what was and is no more. Tears are healthy ways to wash the face. If one grieves a loss and allows the emotions to flow, it is easier to move on. Don't wallow in pain. Wallowing is not moving on. Some of us like to wallow. Why does that feel good? There is an answer. All that we do can be understood as serving our needs in some way.

27. Stay away from negative thinkers. Positive thinking may lead to better outcomes for a number of reasons, but what seems most clear, is that negative thinking stymies good action. People who go around with the attitude that nothing good can happen create self-fulfilling prophecies. Believing we can meet our objectives, that our best visions are possible, that our health is improved by our attitude, or that we can reach our ideals, creates an aura of confidence. Actions follow from our thoughts.

28. Build buffers into your life. Buffers are quiet moments between tasks or actions. These moments allow us to reset ourselves, to renew our plan, to make a check of our intentions, and to allow us to breathe. We live in a fast paced world, and busy workers and parents often move stressfully from one thing to another without stopping. Buffers give us pause to reflect. Buffers let us notice the beauty of our world, enjoy and appreciate people, and get us in touch with our souls.

29. Make a list of values and update them every month. Live by them every day. Values guide us. They help us make choices, and formulate important decisions. In a complex society, opportunity provides for satisfaction of our values, or presents new opportunities. By framing a new set of values monthly, we can both reaffirm our ongoing commitments and open up to new possibilities. Post your values someplace where you can see the list everyday to remind you of what is important to you.

30. Stand back, get the whole picture, a larger view. Use the opportunity to examine the internal and external environment you live in. In business there is often a need for a retreat. Retreats are used to build community, to plan, to vision, and to get together in different places with different people than is normally the case. Individuals can also go on retreats, to a beautiful place, a mountain, to a babbling brook in a deep wood, to the oceans, lakes and parks that surround us. The big picture lets us stop and access where we are and where we are going next.

31. Arrange for silence and reflection in your life and work. Reflection is a time to take stock, to assess the past and imagine the future. Many workplaces are noisy and busy. Try to find a rooftop, a quiet corner, a soft chair. Advocate for a silent room where people meditate or rest. At home, turn off the TV set and all music and appliances for five minutes. Create a silent moment in your life and love it.

32. Know what you want and ask for it, but don't be attached to getting it! Asking for what we want is a gift to others. Their guesses about us are destined to be wrong much of the time. Something interesting happens when we ask for what we want. Be careful what you ask for! Sometimes the answer will be "No". But notice, it is hard to just stop with "No". Something usually follows "No", and sometimes it is actually better than what you asked for, so put it out there, but be careful not to be attached to outcome, at least not right away.

33. Say what you mean; do what you say. This comes from Martin Buber by way of Angeles Arrien. When not upheld, it is the single best predictor of conflict in the world. Make the commitment today, and take it one day at a time. Think before you agree to do anything, and only agree if you know you can carry out the commitment.

34. After you think you have done what you can, do a little more. After you've done your best, see if you can do a little better. You'll be surprised.

35. Listen to children.   Smell the roses. While innocence is our heritage, we do have to learn to protect and defend ourselves. The rose is vulnerable to all sorts of destruction, so see it, smell it, touch it.   Notice its pure uniqueness, the vividness of colors. The pure innocence of the child lives in each of us.

36. Love your mother.

37. "Chop wood, carry water." For Ram Dass this meant live your life in the present. Do the simple things that please you and others. Pay attention to these humble tasks. Enjoy life. "Be here, now."

38. "Follow your bliss." Joseph Campbell adds to the simplicity of staying present. Do what matters to you. Get in touch with what you love, and be that.

39. "There are a thousand ways to kneel and kiss the Earth." Rumi asks us to find love and enjoyment inside ourselves. Examine your habits. Are you living on autopilot? Write a poem today. Play the dulcimer. Do what you love to do.

40. "The greatest gift we can give to anyone else is allowing them to see our love towards ourselves. Only through loving ourselves can we feel love and compassion for someone else." Barbara Lee proposes we spend time each day breathing in the beauty of who we are.

41. "The reason someone else bothers you is because they remind you . . . of yourself. Treat your projections on others as a source of insight that reveals a hidden part of yourself. (But) please don't judge yourself, remember you are discovering your real self through this process." B. Lee

42. "Go forth with an open heart, expecting this to be the most miraculous day of your life whatever and whoever comes into your life is meant to be there."   Life is unfolding and so are we.   Pay attention to what is happening around you. Ask what importance new people or events contain for you.

43. How are you at forgiving? When we learn to forgive, we learn to heal. Judgments about us can end. God is forgiving. Shouldn't we be too?

44. Your life is your own movie - you are the story-writer, the director, the producer and the star. You have no one to blame for the outcome of your movie. Just experience, just feel, just be grateful to be alive. The purpose of our life/movie is to allow Love to enter, is to allow love to soften your heart, and not be afraid anymore." B. Lee

45. Live your life as if today were the first day of the last six months of your life. Notice how this way of thinking establishes much more clearly what is really important to you. Notice how people who have had a brush with death or suffered a serious illness have clear priorities.

46. Play Beach Bocce at least once in your life. Read my book, Beach Bocce Champion!

47. Nobody knows all the tips you need. Give yourself a tip that you know you need. You can actually write it on this page!

Postlude

I always read prefaces of books to see what the author is up to. I wonder at the end, if the destination was met. Of course, maybe the only important question is where the book took you!

As your author, I realized one day that this book of tips would never be finished, and it reminded me of the many quotes that suggest that the journey is more important than the destination.

I used to walk through the woods above my house. I followed a path once used by somebody, but not lately. I changed some of the path. I cleaned up around it. I found a place I liked to sit where the sun came through the trees in a certain way. There was a rock I liked to stand on that gave me a different view and that somehow felt like a powerful apex. There was really no destination, only the path.

This list of tips has been like that. I don't walk that path anymore, but I like to think somebody else is using it as their path, changed to make it their journey. Tip 47 is just the next step on the "journey of a thousand miles"

Appendix 1.

The Top 10 Things to Know About Small Businesses in the US

Are you an entrepreneur or small business owner? Are you supporting entrepreneurs and small businesses? [For research purposes, The Office of Advocacy, Small Business Administration (SBA), defines a small business as having fewer than 500 employees.]

1. More people in the US are becoming self-employed as contractors, freelancers or owners of micro-businesses, though conventional jobs still prevail.

Typically 7% in the US are self-employed. Ed Potter, President of the Employment Policy Foundation, predicts this could grow to as much as 10% in the next several years. This seemingly small percentage (10%) equates to millions of workers in a labor force of 146 million. [Source: Dallas Morning News, "Self-employed, freelance workers on the rise in new job market"]

2. Small businesses are environmentally friendly.

They are usually an active part of their community and also provide innovation. Economic research indicates small businesses innovate at twice the rate of large businesses, which often results in environmentally friendly products and technologies. (Source: Advocacy)

3. Small businesses are often clean businesses.

53% of the 22.9 million small businesses in the U.S. are home-based, and sales and service-oriented, which means they have very little potential for harming the environment.

4. Individuals with more education are more likely to become entrepreneurs, and they are also more likely to open a business employing more people.

5. Small firms represent 99.7% of all employer firms, and employ half of all private sector employees.

They employ 39% of high tech workers (such as scientists, engineers and computer workers).

6. Small businesses generate 60-80% of net new jobs annually.

7. Small businesses create more than 50% of non-farm, private gross domestic product (GDP).

8. There is a strong correlation between national economic growth and the level of national entrepreneurial activity in prior years, according to the Global Entrepreneurship Monitor (GEM).

9. Two-thirds of college students intend to be entrepreneurs at some point in their careers.

10. Small businesses produce 13 to 14 times more patents per employee than large patenting firms. These patents are twice as likely as large firm patents to be among the one percent most cited. (Susan Dunn MA.)

www.ingramcontent.com/pod-product-compliance
Lightning Source LLC
Chambersburg PA
CBHW021921170526
45157CB00005B/2130